AMAZON BESTSELLING AUTHORS

Steps To Personal Revival

Concrete Steps That Will Bring Explosive Revival To You and Those Around You

FRANCIS JONAH

&

PRAYER M. MADUEKE

IMPORTANT

My name is Francis Jonah. I believe all things are possible. It is because of this belief that I have achieved so much in life. This belief extends to all. I believe every human being is equipped to succeed in every circumstance, regardless of the circumstance.

I know the only gap that exists between you and what you need to achieve or overcome is knowledge.

People are destroyed for lack of knowledge.

It is for this reason that I write short practical books that are so simple, people begin to experience immediate results as evidenced by the many testimonies I receive on a daily basis for my various books.

This book is no exception. You will obtain results because of it.

Visit my website for powerful articles and materials

www.francisjonah.com

FREE GIFTS

Just to say Thank You for downloading my book, I'd like to give you these books for free.

Download these 4 powerful books today for free and give yourself a great future.

Click Here to Download

Your testimonies will abound. Click Here to see my other books. They have produced many testimonies and I want your testimony to be one too.

Counselling Or Prayer

Send me an email if you need prayer or counsel or you have a question.

Better still if you want to make my acquaintance

My email is drfrancisjonah@gmail.com

Other books by Francis Jonah

<u>3 Day Fasting Challenge: How to receive manifestation of answers</u>

How to Have Outrageous Financial Abundance In No Time:Biblical Principles For Immediate And Overwhelming Financial Success

5 Bible Promises, Prayers and Decrees That Will Give You The Best Year Ever: A book for Shaping Every Year Successfully plus devotional (Book Of Promises 1)

Influencing The Unseen Realm: How to Influence The Spirit Realm for Victory in The Physical Realm(Spiritual Success Books)

Prayer That Works: Taking Responsibility For Answered Prayer

Healing The Sick In Five Minutes:How Anyone Can Heal Any Sickness

The Financial Miracle Prayer

The Best Secret To Answered Prayer

The Believer's Authority(Authority Of The Believer,Power And Authority Of The Believer)

The Healing Miracle Prayer

I Shall Not Die: Secrets To Long Life And Overcoming The Fear of Death

Three Straightforward Steps To Outrageous Financial Abundance: Personal Finance (Finance Made Easy Book 1)

Prayers For Financial Miracles: And 3 Ways To Receive Answers Quickly

Book: 3 Point Blueprint For Building Strong Faith: Spiritual:Religious:Christian:Motivational

How To Stop Sinning Effortlessly

The Power Of Faith-Filled Words

All Sin Is Paid For: An Eye Opening Book

Be Happy Now:No More Depression

The Ultimate Christian: How To Win In Every Life Situation: A book full of Revelations

Books:How To Be Free From Sicknesses And Diseases(Divine Health): Divine Health Scriptures

Multiply Your Personal Income In Less Than 30 Days

Ultimate Method To Memorize The Bible Quickly: (How To Learn Scripture Memorization)

Overcoming Emotional Abuse

Passing Exams The Easy Way: 90% and above in exams (Learning Simplified)

Books:Goal Setting For Those In A Hurry To Achieve Fast

Do Something Lest You Do Nothing

Financial Freedom:My Personal Blue-Print Made Easy For Men And Women

Why Men Go To Hell

Budgeting Tools And How My Budget Makes Me More Money

How To Raise Capital In 72 Hours: Quickly and Effectively Raise Capital Easily in Unconventional Ways (Finance Made Easy)

How To Love Unconditionally

Financial Independence: The Simple Path I Used To Wealth

Finding Happiness: The Story Of John Miller: A Christian Fiction

Finance Made Easy (2 Book Series)

Click here to see my author page

DEDICATION

This book is dedicated to Rosina Karley Allotey. My mum and the best thing that ever happened to me.

Your memory will forever remain with me. (16/02/1957 – 24/12/2023)

ABOUT PRAYER M. MADUEKE

Prayer M. Madueke is a notable spiritual warfare expert. From humble beginnings, he has risen through the ranks after serving in national and international capacities.

A dynamic deliverance minister, proclaimer of holiness, and a prolific writer. His works have profited many people around the world, and he has continued to declare that effective prayers of the righteous people availeth much.

Presently he is the founder of Prayer Emancipation Missions. He is happily married to Pastor (Mrs.) Roseline C. Madueke and they are blessed with wonderful children.

TABLE OF CONTENT

    ONE

    TWO

    THREE

    FOUR

    FIVE

    SIX

    SEVEN

INTRODUCTION

Many people lose their fire and zeal for God as the days go by and struggle to be revived although they desperately seek revival.

Their hearts cry out for God as well as heklp from somewhere for them to get back on their feet.

In this book, the two authors combine to bring the believer to the very place of personal revival.

As the beginning of the book brings you an overview and a cry for revival, the latter part of the book lays down a simple plan that will revive every believer seeking revival.

Your wait has ended. Your revival is here.

ONE

Steps to Personal Revival

What is Revival?

To revive means to renew, to bring to life again; what was alive but now dead and needs to be revived. It means to turn to consciousness what was unconscious but became unconscious and need to be turned again to consciousness. It is to bring an inactive person or thing to become active and flourish again. To revive means to be restored to consciousness or to life. It is the restoration of a person or thing from a depressed, inactive or unusual state, to it's original state. Personal revival in spiritual perspective means divine visitation to a person in order to bring him or her from the state of spiritual apathy to a renewed life.

> And Jonah began to enter into the city a day's journey, and he cried, and said, yet forty days, and Nineveh shall be overthrown. So, the people of Nineveh believed God, and proclaimed a fast, and put on sackcloth, from the greatest of them even to the least of them. Who can tell if God will turn and repent, and turn away from his fierce anger, that we perish not? And God saw their works, that they turned from their evil way; and God repented of the evil, that he had said that he would do unto them; and he did it not.
>
> — JONAH 3:4-5, 9, 10

When the great city of Nineveh became wicked, abominable and sinful, God sent Jonah to preach salvation unto them. In obedience, the Ninevites heard the preaching, believed God's word, repented of their sins and proclaimed a fast. They put on sackcloth, from the greatest of them, down to the least. They cried to God, turned away from their sins and God's fierce anger was turned away from them. Revival is to quicken a person or persons, move them to become active and, motivate them to pay more attention to righteousness and Godliness. Revival in spiritual perceptive is a powerful and wide spread outpouring of the Holy Spirit upon people.

> And it shall come to pass afterward, that I will pour out my spirit upon all flesh; and your sons and your daughters shall prophesy, your old men shall dream dreams, your young men shall see visions:
>
> — JOEL 2:28

Revival is turning people back to God, to the right way of life, bring them into joy and the peace of the Lord. It is the visitation of God that changes the moral and spiritual state of a community, city or nation. It is a proclamation by a spiritual leader, the pastor or the elders of the church to renounce sin, evil and to serve the only true God.

> And the king commanded Hilkiah the high priest, and the priests of the second order, and the keepers of the door, to bring forth out of the temple of the Lord all the vessels that were made for Baal, and for the grove, and for all the host of heaven: and he burned them without Jerusalem in the fields of Kidron, and carried the ashes of them unto Bethel. And he put down the idolatrous priests, whom the kings of Judah had ordained to burn incense in the high places in the cities of Judah, and in the places round about Jerusalem; them also that burned incense unto Baal, to the sun, and to the moon, and

to the planets, and to all the host of heaven. And he brought out the grove from the house of the Lord, without Jerusalem, unto the brook Kidron, and burned it at the brook Kidron, and stamped it small to powder, and cast the powder thereof upon the graves of the children of the people. And he breaks down the houses of the sodomites, that were by the house of the Lord, where the women wove hangings for the grove.

— 2 KINGS 23:4-7

Revival comes into the church when a leader of the congregation preaches righteousness, calls the congregation to repentance and forsaking their sins with prayers. It is a time to remove spiritually or physically everything in life, in the church that takes the place of the true God. True revival always comes when leaders take the lead against bowing down to images, worshipping images, sacrificing to other gods, worshipping the true God with an image. Most times, true revival comes when people denounce their involvements in occultism, witchcrafts or worshipping of the host of heaven.

> Nebuchadnezzar the king made an image of gold, whose height was threescore cubits, and the breadth thereof six cubits: he set it up in the plain of Dura, in the province of Babylon. And whoso falleth not down and worshippeth shall the same hour be cast into the midst of a burning fiery furnace. Then the king promoted Shadrach, Meshach, and Abednego, in the province of Babylon.
> — DANIEL 3:1, 6, 30

Once upon a time, a King named Nebuchadnezzar made an image and commanded all the princes, the governors, the captains, the judges, the treasurers, the counsellors, the sheriffs, and everyone on earth to bow and worship the image. At that time, he was the president of the whole world made up of about one hundred and twenty-seven provinces in the then known world. All complied except three Hebrew children called Shadrack, Meshach and Abednego. These three boys were brought before the king but they vowed never to bow down to an image. They believed in the deliverance that comes from God, the only true God and vowed that even without deliverance, they would never worship any man-made image or God. At that point, the King was filled with fury and the form of his visage was changed against these three Hebrew boys. He gave an express command to heat the furnace seven times more. Thereafter, he commanded the mightiest men that were in his army to bind them and they did. They were cast into the burning fiery furnace, bound in their coats, their hosen, their hats, other garments and were cast into the midst of the burning fiery furnace. The fire being too hot, slew those men that took them into it but the three boys were loosed in the midst of fire, accompanied by the fourth person untouched by the fire. When King

Nebuchadnezzar saw them alive in the midst of fire, he called them the servants of the highest God. In addition, the princes, governors, captains and the counsellors saw these three men, upon whose bodies the fire had no power over, nor was a single hair on their head burnt. Their coats did not change, nor smell of fire passed on them.

> Then Nebuchadnezzar spake, and said, Blessed be the God of Shadrach, Meshach, and Abednego, who hath sent his angel, and delivered his servants that trusted in him, and have changed the king's word, and yielded their bodies, that they might not serve nor worship any god, except their own God. Therefore, I make a decree, that every people, nation, and language, which speak anything amiss against the God of Shadrach, Meshach, and Abednego, shall be cut in pieces, and their houses shall be made a dunghill: because there is no other God that can deliver after this sort.

— DANIEL 3:28-29

Without much preaching, Nebuchadnezzar said, "Blessed be the God of Shadrack, Meshack and Abednego who sent his angel to deliver his trusted servants." The faith, prayers and actions of these three men reversed the decree of the King and promoted the three Hebrews children that stood for God and Him alone. Shortly before the coming of Christ, the entire world was spiritually dead and it seemed as though God had abandoned the world for Satan to rule and reign in the affairs of men. The Congregation of God, the sanctuary, God's place of fellowship with his children was taken over by the devil and his agents. The chief priests, the elders, chief captains and the governors were possessed by the devil and became massively corrupt. Many Godly leaders, holy ministers were killed violently, poisoned or removed from their positions to suffer hardship, poverty and death. Few of them like Zachariah, Elisabeth his wife, virgin Mary, Joseph,

Simeon, Anna, a prophetess were allowed to minister in the church but with reproach, shame and disgrace after many spiritual attacks.

> There was in the days of Herod, the king of Judaea, a certain priest named Zacharias, of the course of Abia: and his wife was of the daughters of Aaron, and her name was Elisabeth. And they were both righteous before God, walking in all the commandments and ordinances of the Lord blameless. And they had no child, because that Elisabeth was barren, and they both were now well stricken in years. To a virgin espoused to a man whose name was Joseph, of the house of David; and the virgin's name was Mary. And the angel said unto her, Fear not, Mary: for thou hast found favor with God. And, behold, thou shalt conceive in thy womb, and bring forth a son, and shalt call his name Jesus.
>
> — LUKE 1:5-7, 27, 30-31

In the days of Herod, just like our days today, Zachariah and his wife Elisabeth were determined to live righteous in the midst of their defiled generation. They walked in all the commandments and ordinances of the Lord and were found blameless. Even with their righteousness, they had no child because the devil and his agents attacked them with bareness to their old age. Notwithstanding, he executed the priest's office before God in the order of his course. He did everything according to the custom of the priest's office. He never struggled for positions but burnt incense the right way until the day he had divine visitation.

> And, behold, there was a man in Jerusalem, whose name was Simeon; and the same man was just and devout, waiting for the consolation of Israel: and the Holy Ghost was upon him. And it was revealed unto him by the Holy Ghost, that he should not see death,

before he had seen the Lord's Christ. And he came by the Spirit into the temple: and when the parents brought in the child Jesus, to do for him after the custom of the law, Then took he him up in his arms, and blessed God, and said, Lord, now lettest thou thy servant depart in peace, according to thy word: For mine eyes have seen thy salvation, And there was one Anna, a prophetess, the daughter of Phanuel, of the tribe of Aser: she was of a great age, and had lived with an husband seven years from her virginity; And she was a widow of about fourscore and four years, which departed not from the temple, but served God with fasting and prayers night and day. And she coming in that instant gave thanks likewise unto the Lord, and spake of him to all them that looked for redemption in Jerusalem.

— LUKE 2:25-30, 36-38

Joseph in his own way of life and Virgin Mary were engaged to get married but decided to keep themselves holy, undefiled till the day they had angelic visitation. Virgin Mary knowing fully well that she was a sinner who needed a savior like every other human remained humble, prayerful and visited Elisabeth (Luke 1:40, 46-56). These five faithful believers and possibly a few others according to my understanding came together often and prayed for revival in their generation, in the days of Herod. I strongly believe that Psalm 74 was written between the last book of Old Testament and the New Testament (Psalm 74:1-23).

TWO

Mark of Spiritual Decay

Our generation is in serious need of revival much more than the days of Herod and every believer is called to take up the challenge. Our generation is a time, a period marked by evil, dominion of Satan and darkness. We are living face to face with a period of time marked with ungodliness, lusts, denial of Christ, denial of faith, sound doctrine and denial of Christ's return (Galatians 1:4; 2 Corinthians 4:4; Ephesians 6:12; Luke 17:26; 1 John 2:18; 1 Timothy 4:1-4; 2 Timothy 3:4). When believers, church workers especially ministers has started to experience formality and insensibility to the voice of the Holy Ghost, we must pray for revival. The visibility of mechanical spiritual life in many churches today has increased, pointing to us that we need revival.

> And she said, The Philistines be upon thee, Samson. And he awoke out of his sleep, and said, I will go out as at other times before, and shake myself. And he knew not that the Lord was departed from him.
> — JUDGES 16:20

Many ministers are engaged in activities, programs that doesn't promote the spirituality of their members. We are experiencing carnality in many ministers' personal lifestyles and lack of brotherly true love. Many congregations are filled with dissension, jealousy, envy, in fighting and evil speaking against one another. In these last days, God is warning the church against the explosion of false cults, counterfeits and idolatry. The church of our time is filled with backslidden Samsons who know not that the Lord has departed from them. Many of them are still operating but with jealousy, greed, immorality, covetousness, pride, anger and in evil competitions.

> For such are false apostles, deceitful workers, transforming themselves into the apostles of Christ. And no marvel; for Satan himself is transformed into an angel of light. Therefore, it is no great thing if his ministers also be transformed as the ministers of righteousness; whose end shall be according to their works.
>
> — 2 CORINTHIANS 11:13-15

The Wrong Steps to Modern Revival.

(Psalm 74:1-23)

Paul was not comfortable with the spiritual decay in the Corinthian church from the beginning. The church was filled with false apostles, teachers and lying wonders that looked like miracles. In his second epistle to them, his fear was that Satan, the serpent has beguiled them like he did to Eve. Many in the church were preaching another Christ in a deceitful manner, transformed as apostle of Christ. In our generation church today, many has gone out to get fake powers from the devil to deceive many. They prophesy, tell lies, transfer problems, suspend demonic activities, confuse people with temporary prosperities without righteousness.

> There was a certain rich man, which was clothed in purple and fine linen, and fared sumptuously every day: And it came to pass, that the beggar died, and was carried by the angels into Abraham's bosom: the rich man also died, and was buried; And in hell he lift up his eyes, being in torments, and seeth Abraham afar off, and Lazarus in his bosom.
> — LUKE 16:19, 22-23

In today's generation, many churches, ministers promote temporary blessings above spiritual blessings (John 6:10-15, 25-35, 60, 66; Psalm 106:13-16). They preach and lead their deceived members to pursue prosperity and abundance without righteousness (Deuteronomy 32:5, 6, 15; Jeremiah 22:21, 22; Revelation 3:14-20). I was told of a minister who usually visited witch doctors, enter satanic temple and altars, just to gather large members during his special programs. Some receive demonic anointed tongues to speak and whatever they say, their hearers obey without question only to regret later. They have their tongues, ears and eyes anointed demonically to perform fake miracles that doesn't last. They don't cast out demons but are in covenant with the devil to suspend, postpone or transfer problems for a certain period of time. In order to maintain their fake anointing, they do abominable things. Many of them engage in unimaginable sexual perversions, extreme wicked sacrifices, do anything to get money, prophesy falsely, promote strange doctrines, trade with their members destinies and live flamboyant lifestyles.

> And it came to pass, as we went to prayer, a certain damsel possessed with a spirit of divination met us, which brought her masters much gain by soothsaying: And when her masters saw that the hope of their gains was gone, they caught Paul and Silas, and drew them into the marketplace unto the rulers,
>
> — ACTS 16:16, 19

> So, I prophesied as I was commanded: and as I prophesied, there was a noise, and behold a shaking, and the bones came together, bone to his bone. And when I beheld, lo, the sinews and the flesh came up upon them, and the skin covered them above: but there was no breath in them.

— EZEKIEL 37:7, 8

In their fellowships, you hear the noise of singing, clapping, shaking, drumming and dancing without divine life in them. They are dead spiritually, bones filled with flesh without the breath of life. Ezekiel prophesied and the bones came together with flesh but there was no breath from God. Many of our leaders, church workers come to church looking beautiful, with beautiful make ups, and glittering skins, shaking, drumming and dancing without God's breath in them. Business prosperities, car dedications, house warming and all manner of prosperities are good but worse without God and his divine breath in them. Your good make up, nice appearance, financial and material breakthroughs may cover your sin without spiritual life (1 Corinthians 3:1; 5:1-8). Carnality, spiritual immaturity, immorality and sin with the manifestation of your so-called miracles is useless and unprofitable before divine measures.

THREE

Price for Personal Revival

In every generation, God is always looking for men who He will use to start revival in the dying communities, cities and nations. Men that can lock and unlock, bind and loose to start revival in this generation are badly needed by God. Men He can empower with supernatural power with saintly purpose and sound principles to pray until revival comes.

> The people of the land have used oppression, and exercised robbery, and have vexed the poor and

needy: yea, they have oppressed the stranger wrongfully. And I sought for a man among them, that should make up the hedge, and stand in the gap before me for the land, that I should not destroy it: but I found none.

— EZEKIEL 22:29, 30

God is perpetually searching for men and women to put his revival spirit in them to turn the tables against the devil in this generation. God is placing a call upon you to be used to revive the church, the cities and nations to terminate the oppression going on everywhere here on earth. There are lots of intimidation, manipulations and bewitchment going on all over the world and God is searching for you to be used. Many poor people whose names are in the book of life with great needs are being denied of their rights and God wants you to stand up in the gap. God is searching for men and women of self-denial, consecrated, renewed and fervent in prayers to bring revival again. Men and women who are prepared to enter into the burning fiery furnace and come out with the fourth man in the fire. One of the prices to pay is to overcome the fire of tongues in your church, office and your community.

> Even so the tongue is a little member, and boasteth great things. Behold, how great a matter a little fire kindleth! And the tongue is a fire, a world of iniquity: so is the tongue among our members, that it defileth the whole body, and setteth on fire the course of nature; and it is set on fire of hell.
> — JAMES 3:5, 6

> An ungodly man diggeth up evil: and in his lips there is as a burning fire. A froward man soweth strife: and a whisperer separateth chief friends. A violent man enticeth his neighbor, and leadeth him into the way that is not good. He shutteth his eyes to devise

froward things: moving his lips he bringeth evil to pass.

— PROVERBS 16:27-30

Sometimes, the witches, wizards and, enemies of righteousness against Godly revival will release demonic spirits in the tongues of people around you. They may open their mouth, use their tongues to tell all manner of lies, frame you up, bear false witnesses against you and everyone will believe them. The devil against godly preparations for a revival may enter into your friends, enemies, church leadership and office people against you. They may boast, threaten you, petition you and determine to destroy your faith. They may attack you with occultic fire, strange sicknesses, agents of defilements and all manner of threats against your faith in Christ. No matter what happens, you must pay the price of revival and remain in faith (Proverbs 26:18-26).

Thou shalt be hid from the scourge of the tongue: neither shalt thou be afraid of destruction when it cometh.

— JOB 5:21

Thou shalt hide them in the secret of thy presence from the pride of man: thou shalt keep them secretly in a pavilion from the strife of tongues.

— PSALM 31:20

The world we are living in is filled with strange fire, evil arrows, deceits, strife, contentions, wickedness and hatred because of multiple evil sacrifices that invokes demons. If you must be used to start a revival in this generation full of evil tongues, you must overcome deception, slander, conspiracies, criticism, betrayal, contention and division from the demonic world. Those that God will use to spark up revival this end time must pass through the fire of persecution and opposition in and outside the church.

> I am come to send fire on the earth; and what will I, if it be already kindled? But I have a baptism to be baptized with; and how am I straitened till it be accomplished! Suppose ye that I am come to give peace on earth? I tell you, Nay; but rather division: For from henceforth there shall be five in one house divided, three against two, and two against three. The father shall be divided against the son, and the son against the father; the mother against the daughter, and the daughter against the mother; the mother-in-law against her daughter in law, and the daughter in law against her mother-in-law.
>
> — LUKE 12:49-53

If you have the Spirit of Christ, the unbelievers, sinners around you will see you as a trouble maker. You will be persecuted for standing for Christ and will be tested, tried and proved as a true child of God. You will always be singled out in the midst of others for standing aloof for the truth without compromise. Your trusted friends, blood relations and colleagues will fight your decision for Christ.

> But the Lord hath taken you, and brought you forth out of the iron furnace, even out of Egypt, to be unto him a people of inheritance, as ye are this day.
>
> — DEUTERONOMY 4:20

Therefore, they did set over them taskmasters to afflict them with their burdens. And they built for Pharaoh treasure cities, Pithom and Raamses. But the more they afflicted them, the more they multiplied and grew. And they were grieved because of the children of Israel. And the Egyptians made the children of Israel to serve with rigor: And they made their lives bitter with hard bondage, in mortar, and in brick, and in all manner of service in the field: all their service, wherein they made them serve, was with rigor.

— EXODUS 1:11-14

Your faith in God will be put to test in difficult situations under iron furnace in the midst of the troubled sea. Evil monitors, spiritually and physically will be raised against you to monitor your activities under heavy afflictions. The devil and his agents will attack you from every side with merciless afflictions, multiple troubles to cause you to deny your faith. You may be grieved from every side, caused to serve with rigor with bitter bondage in and outside your neighborhood. In times like this, when many Christians are giving up because of oppression, injustice, poverty, denial of fundamental rights, you are under test and called to stand for God. Many Christians all over the world are being tested, tried in the church and in the world but you are expected to stand for Christ for divine selection for end time revival. Many are suffering now in churches, outside the church, in their place of work, made slaves, under universal humiliation but you must not give up your faith. You need to cheer up and pray for revival. There are many trials, troubles but remember, they are called light afflictions. If you remain faithful, loyal and obedient to God's eternal, unchanging truth, His power will protect you and preserve you to partake in the end time revival (Isaiah 43:1, 2; Psalm 34:19; 2 Timothy 4:18; 2 Corinthians 12:19; Daniel 3:21-30). With the strength and God's grace, you will overcome by closely following the word of God. In the time of Herod, Zachariah, his wife Elisabeth, in the days of King Herod, they both remained righteous before God. In the time when other ministers, believers compromised their faith, they walked in all the commandment and ordinances of God and remained blameless. Under witchcraft attacks of barrenness, they were stricken for years, but they served God according to the custom. Together with the few remaining believers like Joseph, Virgin Mary, Simeon and Anna, they prayed for revival, divine visitations till the day their prayers were answered.

> O God, why hast thou cast us off forever? why doth thine anger smoke against the sheep of thy pasture? Remember thy congregation, which thou hast purchased of old; the rod of thine inheritance, which thou hast redeemed; this mount Zion, wherein thou hast dwelt. Lift up thy feet unto the perpetual desolations; even all that the enemy hath done wickedly in the sanctuary.
> — PSALM 74:1-3

They cried to God, prayed that God should visit the congregation, the rod of his inheritance, his redeemed under afflictions. In the midst of corrupt ministers, defiled generation, Zachariah and Elisabeth cried to God for revival. In the midst of defiled youths, Virgin Mary and Joseph remained virgins, undefiled. In the midst of corrupt senior ministers, general overseers, church leaders, unjust father in the lords, prayerless priests, Simeon remained just, devoted, waiting for divine revival. When deaths descended upon other aged ministers, he refused to die but prayed and fought against death until he saw the Lord Christ. In the midst of false prophetess, evil seers, polluted widows in the house of God, Anna remained a virgin to the day she got married. Though, she lost her husband after seven years of marriage, she refused to defile herself with the pastors, rich and wealthy believers in the congregation and the politicians. For eighty-four years, she kept herself holy, took the office of intercession in the temple, served God with fasting and prayers night and day till her day of revival came. She was among the prayer warriors who prayed against evil ministers, occultic Old Testament elders, evil chief priests who served the devil in the congregation of her time. She payed the price of revival by praying against the activities of the enemies of God, who roared in the midst of the congregations with fake powers.

> Thine enemies roar in the midst of thy congregations; they set up their ensigns for signs. A man was famous according as he had lifted up axes upon the thick trees. But now they break down the carved work thereof at once with axes and hammers.
> — PSALM 74:4-6

She was among the few believers in the time of Herod, occult ministers with counterfeit powers (Exodus 7:10-13, 20-22; 8:5-7, 16-19; 1 Kings 22:6-8, 12, 20-23; 1 Samuel 18:10, 11; Ezekiel 9:1-4; Revelation 13:11-17; 2 Thessalonians 2:7-12).

To my understanding, Zachariah, Elisabeth, Joseph, Virgin Mary, Simeon, Anna and possible few others usually gather to pray for revival and the termination of occultic revival in the house of God. Their prayers must have been centered against the activities of the evil priests, ministers, and wealthy evil elders who changed God's signs to ensigns, organized programs, and used the name of God to make money.

> They have cast fire into thy sanctuary, they have defiled by casting down the dwelling place of thy name to the ground. They said in their hearts, let us destroy them together: they have burned up all the synagogues of God in the land. We see not our signs: there is no more any prophet: neither is there among us any that knoweth how long.
>
> — PSALM 74:7-9

Their prayers must have been focused against the evil activities of the occultic politicians, evil leaders in the congregation who used human brains to prosper, became famous, and much gain. (Acts 16:16, 19). In many churches today, God's presence to deliver, heal the sick and prosper true believers are scarce. All that we see is occultic witchcrafts manifestations, evil changes, magicians and threats against the righteous. Many corrupt leaders are been respected above God and their fear is beyond explanation. They sit in God's place, act like God, practice wickedness in the sanctuary without a challenge. They became famous, rich, and very powerful by practicing witchcrafts, occultism, divination, charms and destroying the righteous. Many in the church who question their evil actions are attacked with strange burning fires in their bodies, marriages, business and the destructions of their children. God's true miracles, signs, wonders are replaced with ensigns, bewitchments and evil authorities.

> O God, how long shall the adversary reproach? shall the enemy blaspheme thy name forever? Remember thy congregation, which thou hast purchased of old; the rod of thine inheritance, which thou hast redeemed; this mount Zion, wherein thou hast dwelt.

> Remember this, that the enemy hath reproached, O Lord, and that the foolish people have blasphemed thy name. Forget not the voice of thine enemies: the tumult of those that rise up against thee increaseth continually.
>
> — PSALM 74:10, 2, 18, 23

This is the time for believers and the remaining contending ministers to cry for revival, personally and congregationally. This is the time for true believers to pray for divine intervention, end of evil reign and satanic reproaches in our midst. Our God has not changed, neither is He partial or weak in taking action against satanic reign or rule. When Zachariah and Elisabeth prayed in the days of Herod, they received angelic visitation (Luke 1:11-25). Through divine visitation, John the Baptist was born and the revival started through his ministry. When Virgin Mary and Joseph prayed, angel Gabriel was sent to their house with answers to their prayers that gave birth to our savior, the

Lord Jesus. When Simeon prayed, he received a revelation that he will not test death until he sees Jesus, take Him to his arms and blessed God. Death avoided him until he fulfilled his ministry with his eyes opened to see the salvation and revival in Israel. Anna likewise remained holy, pure for eighty-four years, serving God in the temple with prayers and fasting, night and day until the day her prayers were answered with great revival. These are men and women who paid the price for revival, met the required results and took the steps to revival. Today you are called to join the few believers who are still contending for the faith and praying for personal revival. If you are not yet born again, you can join the chariot by repenting and confessing your sins.

> And Samuel spake unto all the house of Israel, saying, if ye do return unto the Lord with all your hearts, then put away the strange gods and Ashtaroth from among you, and prepare your hearts unto the Lord, and serve him only: and he will deliver you out

> of the hand of the Philistines. Then the children of Israel did put away Baalim and Ashtaroth, and served the Lord only.
>
> — 1 SAMUEL 7:3, 4

No matter your denomination, you can repent now, despise your differences, confess your sins and forsake them to pray for personal and congregational revival. To make progress, idols must not be allowed in your heart. All unforgiven spirits must be expunged and strained relationships must be dealt with. Deal with impure motives, evil desires, all immoral responses, evil imaginations and thoughts that has overtaken you.

FOUR

WARFARE SECTION:

3 Days Prayers Of Decrees For Global Revival

Day 1

Anything in me fighting against God's will for my life, receive destruction, in the mighty name of Jesus. Almighty God, empower me to live above sin, and its consequences all the days of my life, in the name of Jesus. I break and loose myself from every anti-revival demon, in the name of Jesus. Almighty God, empower me to pay the price of personal revival, in the name of Jesus. Every yoke of defilement and pollution in my life, break to pieces, in the name of Jesus. Any evil program, organized to separate me from God's plan, fail woefully, in the name of Jesus. Father Lord, qualify me for personal revival, in the mighty name of Jesus. Ancient of days, deliver me from the consequences of my foundational bondage, in the name of Jesus. I break and loose myself from every evil relationship, in the name of Jesus. Almighty God, disengage me from every evil movement assigned to discredit me from personal revival, in the name of Jesus. Heavenly father, plant the nine fruits and gifts of your Spirit in my life forever and empower me to be revived by your Spirit, in the name of Jesus. Every yoke of sin in any area of my life, break to pieces, in the mighty name of Jesus. Blood of Jesus, speak me out of every demonic activity and engage me in your activity forever, in the name of Jesus. Let the blood of Jesus mark me for end time global revival, in the name of Jesus. Blood of Jesus, speak me out of every organized darkness, in the name of Jesus. Father Lord, pour your Spirit upon me and cause me to be revived for your work all the days of my life, in the name of Jesus. Every enemy of the manifestations of God's power in my life, be exposed and disgraced, in the name of Jesus.

Day 2

Let the power of God waste every satanic material in my life, in the name of Jesus. Almighty God, use me to terminate the works of the devil everywhere I go, in the name of Jesus. Let the established unrepentant enemies of God's revival be dethroned in shame, in the name of Jesus. I break and loose myself from the agents of the devil assigned to frustrate God's plans for my life, in the name of Jesus. Every demonic roadblock standing against the manifestations of God's revival, be dismantled, in the name of Jesus. Let the chains of darkness, reproaches and disgrace in the lives of true believers worldwide break to pieces, in the name of Jesus. Let the resurrection power fall upon every believer all over the world, in the name of Jesus. Every spirit of Herod prospering anywhere against God's children, I bind and cast you out, in the name of Jesus. Anointing to prosper believers all over the world for divine revival, fall upon all Christians, in the name of Jesus. Spirit of the living God, manifest in every nation and bring global revival, in the name of Jesus. I terminate every witchcraft spirit in the lives of believers all over the world, in the name of Jesus. Almighty God, more than you did in the city of Nineveh, repeat it all over the nations of the world, in the name of Jesus. Every hindrance to the manifestations of divine revival, disappear forever, in the name of Jesus. Every demonic instrument of sin and manipulation, catch fire and burn to ashes, in the name of Jesus. Father Lord, destroy every enemy of your revival spirit in my life, in the name of Jesus. I command the backbone of sin in the lives of every believer to break to pieces, in the name of Jesus. Almighty God, recruit young and old, male and female believers and revive them in every church, in the name of Jesus. Anointing to raise intercessors that will initiate global revival, fall upon every believer, in the name of Jesus. Every evil gang up against divine revival, scatter in shame, in the name of Jesus. Blood of Jesus, flow into the end and the beginning of the world among the creation and terminate every demonic activity, in the name of Jesus.

Every negative voice or activity speaking against divine revival, be silenced forever by the speaking blood of Jesus. Every throne of witchcraft in every church and government authority, be dethroned, in the name of Jesus.

Day 3

Every satanic agent, evil group against God's revival in this generation, scatter in shame, in the name of Jesus. Anything that must happen for the church to be revived again, begin to happen, in the mighty name of Jesus. Every satanic seat in every nation, catch fire, burn to ashes, in the name of Jesus. Every death that must take place to bring global revival, spiritually or physically, wherever you are, begin to manifest, in the name of Jesus. Let the lives of the revivalist in every nation be prolonged and protected, in the name of Jesus. Almighty God, pour your Spirit of holiness and prayers upon every nation, in the name of Jesus. Almighty God, gather together believers in every nation to start praying for global revival, in the name of Jesus. Let the foundation of Christianity in any nation under arrest be released by force, in the name of Jesus. Any strange fire in the lives of believers and in every church, be quenched by the speaking blood of Jesus. Any evil mark in the lives of every believer worldwide, be cleansed by the blood of

Jesus. Any evil sacrifice ever offered against divine revival, expire and die, in the name of Jesus. Any satanic program, evil movement in the dark world about to stop the move of God in any nation, be terminated, in the name of Jesus. Every enemy of God's righteousness in my life, receive total destruction, in the name of Jesus. I command everyone working against the manifestations of God's revival to repent or perish, in the name of Jesus. Let the men and women of like passion for revival be brought together for prayers of revival, in the name of Jesus. Mass repentance everywhere in the world for global revival, begin to take place from person to person, in the name of Jesus. I command every creature to war against sin and Satan everywhere in the world, in the name of Jesus. Any evil action ever taken and will ever be taken against the manifestations of God's revival, fail woefully, in the name of Jesus. Let the reign of the devil, sin and its consequences against the manifestations of God's righteousness be terminated, in the name of Jesus. Lord Jesus, arise in your power, rule and reign in every nation like never before in this generation, in the name of Jesus.

FIVE

Benefits of Personal Revival

If you have ever wondered why personal revival is important in your life, this chapter will give you the reasons for you to embark on personal revival quickly.

Powerful Prayer life

Personal revival brings such a dimension to your prayer life that you will never imagine existed.

The first sign that tells many people that they need revival in their lives is that their prayer life goes down tremendously.

This is obviously the plan of the enemy to stop you from powering your destiny.

Every believer has power in them and prayer is that which generates and releases the power within us.

This is why things happen when we pray.

Do you remember the story of how Peter escaped from prison after the church prayed for him?

That was power being released through prayer.

That was his destiny being released from negativity into positivity.

> Act 12:5 Peter therefore was kept in prison: but prayer was made without ceasing of the church unto God for him.
>
> Acts 12:5

The prayer of the church was constant. This is what released the power that brought Peter out of prison.

Your prayer life becomes powerful and result producing when you are revived.

This is the account of the deliverance of Peter:

Act 12:7 And, behold, the angel of the Lord came upon him, and a light shined in the prison: and he smote Peter on the side, and raised him up, saying, Arise up quickly. And his chains fell off from his hands.

Act 12:8 And the angel said unto him, Gird thyself, and bind on thy sandals. And so he did. And he saith unto him, Cast thy garment about thee, and follow me.

Act 12:9 And he went out, and followed him; and wist not that it was true which was done by the angel; but thought he saw a vision.

Act 12:10 When they were past the first and the second ward, they came unto the iron gate that leadeth unto the city; which opened to them of his own accord: and they went out, and passed on through one street; and forthwith the angel departed from him.

Act 12:11 And when Peter was come to himself, he said, Now I know of a surety, that the Lord hath sent his angel, and hath delivered me out of the hand of

> Herod, and from all the expectation of the people of the Jews.

The miracle of his release surprised Peter so much that he didn't even believe this was happening to him.

That is what revival does to you. It gives you a powerful result producing prayer life.

The devil has a field day when the people of God are not praying.

Remember that he is going about like a roaring lion seeking someone to devour.

He is looking for a prey.

He is looking for someoene who is down in prayer to make a captive and a victiom of circumstamces.

He is looking for someone to steal from, to kill and to destroy.

When you receive personal revival, you can never be that person.

You live above the terrain of his victims.

> 1Pe 5:8 Be sober, be vigilant; because your adversary the devil, as a roaring lion, walketh about, seeking whom he may devour:
>
> 1 Peter 5:8

The Psalmist summarized the effect of revival on prayer in these words:

> Psa 80:18 So will not we go back from thee: quicken us, and we will call upon thy name.
>
> Psalm 80:18

When you quicken us, we will call upon your name. In other words, when you revive us, we will pray.
That is the first benefit of personal revival. Let us proceed to the next benefit.

Separation from sin and the unclean
The next benefit of personal revival is that it separates you from sin and unclean things.

When you are unrevived and down in your spiritual life, it is easy for you to fall into sin and indulge in all kinds of activities that grieve the Spirit of God.

The Bible is clear that the formula for a man or woman to cleanse his or her ways is to have the word of God in them.

When you are revived, you have the privilege and hunger to study the word of God all the time.

This helps you keep your thoughts and your ways pure.

Anyone who has been without revival will tell you how difficult it is to study the Bible.

For this reason that which cleanses them and holds them in check is missing out fo their lives.

David was so much aware of this and that is why he said:

> Psa 119:11 Thy word have I hid in mine heart, that I might not sin against thee.
>
> Psalm 119:11

The word helps us not to sin.

The word helps us live on a pedestal that is so high above sin and the unclean.

That is the pedestal you will walk in when you are revived.

It is a benefit revival bestows on anyone who is revived.

Revival also helps you tap into the benefit of the cleansing power of the word.

The scriptures are clear on that. The focus revival gives you on God alone helps you keep your mind stayed on him and not the mundane things of the world. This is how David described the power of the word of God:

> Psa 119:9 BETH. Wherewithal shall a young man cleanse his way? by taking heed thereto according to thy word.
>
> Psalm 119:9

Revival thus separates you from sin and its effects as well as all unclean things that serve as weights in your journey in life.

When these weights are lifted, you become free to move faster and accomplish greater things while hosting the presence of God in greater dimensions.

Rewards of soul winning

When you are revived, soul winning becomes a part of your itinerary.

Anyone who is engaged in soul winning is practically storing rewards in the kingdom of heaven.

Jesus was express in his command to us. He told us to make disciples of all nations. This means we must be able to go out and speak to people.

We must teach them and make sure they have received the salvation of God.

> Mat 28:19 Go ye therefore, and teach all nations, baptizing them in the name of the Father, and of the Son, and of the Holy Ghost:
>
> Matthew 28:19

When we do this, we receive rewards from God in heaven when we get there.

The earth is not the home of believers. It is a temporary place of pilgrimage. There is a whole eternity for us to live and we are not living it in this temporary body.

There are souls that are perishing and God expects us to save them through the preaching of the gospel. Understand that he that wins souls is wise because such a person is storing up treasure in heaven:

> Pro 11:30 The fruit of the righteous is a tree of life; and he that winneth souls is wise.
>
> Proverbs 11:30

When you are revived, soul winning becomes a part of your very nature. You are eager to preach. You are eager to win souls.

You are eager to save the lost at all cost.

Paul got to this place and he said boldy:

> Rom 1:16 For I am not ashamed of the gospel of Christ: for it is the power of God unto salvation to every one that believeth; to the Jew first, and also to the Greek.
>
> Romans 1:16

When you are revived, you are not ashamed of the gospel. You preach it at work, you preach it in the bus, you preach it in the market place. As a matter of truth, you preach it wherever you have opportunity.

Jesus boldy said we should store our treasure in heaven. It means as we work, we store up treasure in heaven:

> Mat 6:19 Lay not up for yourselves treasures upon earth, where moth and rust doth corrupt, and where thieves break through and steal:
>
> Mat 6:20 But lay up for yourselves treasures in heaven, where neither moth nor rust doth corrupt, and where thieves do not break through nor steal:

Matthew 6:19-20

When you are revived, you will put in the work that will cause you to excel and obtain rewards as a Christian.

Revival of other believers

Another great benefit of being revived is that, your revival tends to affect other believers.

When your prayer life is vibrant, it affects other prayer lives.

When your fasting life is vibrant it influences other people to start fasting too.

When your Bible study and meditation is on fire, it puts a check on other people who also begin to follow suit.

The book of Proverbs was right on this account:

> Pro 27:17 Iron sharpeneth iron; so a man sharpeneth the countenance of his friend.
>
> Proverbs 27:17

There are many people who have experienced their fair share of revival because people around them were revived.

Personally, I know of many people who were revived because I received revival of my own. Some of them went on to become pastors and are doing great things in the kingdom.

Your revival can affect an individual, a family, a town or even a generation.

No one can put a limit to what your revival can bring.

The story of the woman at the well comes to mind so easily. When she encounered Jesus, her whole town encountered him too.

> Joh 4:28 The woman then left her waterpot, and went her way into the city, and saith to the men,
>
> Joh 4:29 Come, see a man, which told me all things that ever I did: is not this the Christ?

> Joh 4:30 Then they went out of the city, and came unto him.
>
> John 4:28-30

This whole town received a revival because of one woman.

That is the power your personal revival can carry. This is the reason you must not give up on being revived as a person.

Walking in the supernatural

When you are revived, walking in the supernatural becomes very easy.

Doing great and mighty things in the spirit come easily when you are revived. You begin to fulfil the mandate given to us by Jesus Christ himself:

> Mar 16:17 And these signs shall follow them that believe; In my name shall they cast out devils; they shall speak with new tongues;

> Mar 16:18 They shall take up serpents; and if they drink any deadly thing, it shall not hurt them; they shall lay hands on the sick, and they shall recover.
>
> Mark 16:17-18

This is a mandate given to all believers, yet many of us are falling short of it. That inactivity becomes a thing of the past when revival hits an individual.

The gospel is preached, the sick are healed and the dead are raised. All this is done with enthusiasm just because of the effects of revival.

Indeed, Jesus made us understand that we are supposed to do certain things because he had given us the power to do so.

That power is dormant within many people. These signs must follow us. They must be evident wherever we are as believers.

May revival come upon your life so that you will manifest these great signs to the glory of God.

> Mat 10:7 And as ye go, preach, saying, The kingdom of heaven is at hand.
>
> Mat 10:8 Heal the sick, cleanse the lepers, raise the dead, cast out devils: freely ye have received, freely give.
>
> Matthew 10:7-8

These benefits of revival can spread from a person to a whole community and the world at large. It starts with one person.

Now that you are aware of the benefits of revival, let us look at the ingredients that come together to bring forth revival.

SIX
Ingredients For Personal Revival

There are certain ingredients that come together to spark personal revival.

These ingredients are such that when incorporated into the life of a believer, revival has no option than to erupt.

In this chapter, we will delve into each of these ingredients to make sure that you fully understand them.

Repentance

The first ingredient for true personal revival is a turning away from all apearance of evil.

This is what repentance entails.

There are many believers who have become comfortable with evil. This comfort has become a great hindrance to revival in their lives.

The Bible is clear about evil:

> 1Th 5:22 Abstain from all appearance of evil.
>
> **1 Thessalonians 5:22**

This is a deep scripture. We are not asked to abstain from evil but even the very appearance of it.

This is a deeper level of repentance and turning away.

For revival to erupt in your life, you must take stock of the things that do not please God in your life and turn away from them with the help of the Holy Spirit.

Decisions and consecrations

There are certain decisions and consecrations that will aid personal revival in your life.

These may look like small decisions but can go a long way to charge up your spiritual life.

Many great men have made certain decisions and consecrations that have taken them from one level of glory to the other.

Job opens our eyes to one of such consecrations:

> Job 31:1 I made a covenant with mine eyes; why then should I think upon a maid?
>
> **Job 31:1**

Among the consecrations others have made are:

1. Rejecting every lustful thought immediately it comes
2. Not reading the newspaper
3. Not keeping offence in their heart over one day
4. Not witholding their money from God
5. Not going a day without prayer
6. Not going one week without fasting
7. Speaking the truth no matter what
8. Preaching to win a soul every week
9. Preserving physical and spiritual purity

10. Meditating on scriptures daily

These simple decisions and consecrations have made many people great and deepened their relationship and fellowship with God.

Many people have attributed their spiritual success to the consecrations of their life.

It is very important to establish your own consecrations for your next level spiritually.

Prayer

Prayer is a major ingredient of revival.

There is no revival that took place without the element of revival.

It is the very vehicle by which people come to the presence of God.

The investment of prayer is what sparks revival in every generation. Therefore for personal revival, it is absolutely necessary that prayer is also invested.

God made this clear to the people of Israel:

2Ch 7:14 If my people, which are called by my name, shall humble themselves, and pray, and seek my face, and turn from their wicked ways; then will I hear from heaven, and will forgive their sin, and will heal their land.

2 Chronicles 7:14

God clearly made His people understand that prayer preceded His move in their lives.

This is why prayer is a key ingredient when it comes to personal revival.

You ignore it at your own peril. Make time for prayer, let it be part of your daily schedule and you will always be on fire.

The next key ingredient to personal revival is fasting

Fasting

Jesus was an advocate of fasting and prayer when it came to overcoming obstacles and receiving inner strength.

He said so in the the book of Matthew:

> Mat 17:21 Howbeit this kind goeth not out but by prayer and fasting.
>
> Matthew 17:21

Throughout the Bible, fasting has been used as a means to draw closer to God.

Many people who have strayed away have used fasting as a means of quickening their journey back to God.

This is what the town of Nineveh did when they had incurred the anger of God:

> Jon 3:5 So the people of Nineveh believed God, and proclaimed a fast, and put on sackcloth, from the greatest of them even to the least of them.
>
> **Jonah 3:5**

For revival to spring forth in your life, you need the ingredeient of fasting.

Once you can incorportae it in your life, personal revival will be an experience you will enjoy all the time.

It is a cornerstone that has worked wonders for long.

The next key ingredient is the word of God.

The word

The word of God is food for your spirit. It brings vitality to your life as a believer and sparks revival with the inspiration it releases to the believer.

Every believer who wants to enjoy revival must keep the word of God close.

The Psalmist emphasized the role of the word of God in remaining fresh as a believer.

> Psa 1:2 But his delight is in the law of the LORD; and in his law doth he meditate day and night.

Psa 1:3 And he shall be like a tree planted by the rivers of water, that bringeth forth his fruit in his season; his leaf also shall not wither; and whatsoever he doeth shall prosper.

Psalm 1:1-2

With meditation in the word, your spiritual life does not wither.

You are always revived looking for who next to impact.

This is why it is very important to add the reading and meditation of the word of God in your schedule.

The importance of this spiritual exercise cannot be underestimated.

Let us now talk about keeping your revival fire alive.

SEVEN

Keeping Revival Fire Alive

The key to keeping revival fire alive is to plan a sessions of revibval ahead of time.

Planning is essential so that your fire doesn't come down before you struggle to keep it up again.

Once you have a program of personal revival drawn out, you are on your way to living a revived life all year round.

Some people engage the ingredients of revival every day.

Some engage them every week, some engage these ingredients every month in varying proportions.

You need to determine which mix helps you best and then you apply it.

Thus someones plan to keep revival fire burning can be:

Plan One

1. Read one chapter daily
2. Pray an hour daily
3. Fast twice a week
4. Walk in my consecrations daily and repent if I fall short of any.
5. Major fasting and prayer for three days every month

Plan Two

1. Read two chapters daily
2. Pray two hours daily
3. Fast twice a month(every other Sunday)
4. Walk in my consecrations daily and repent if I fall short of any
5. Major fasting and prayer for three days every month(first three days of the month)

By planning for the year, you can keep your revival fire burning all year long.

At this juncture, I can confidently say that you are ready to be revived as well as release revival fire to all others around you.

FREE GIFTS

Just to say Thank You for downloading my book, I'd like to give you these books for free.

Download these 4 powerful books today for free and give yourself a great future.

Click Here to Download

Your testimonies will abound. Click <u>Here</u> to see my other books. They have produced many testimonies and I want your testimony to be one too.

Other books by Francis Jonah

3 Day Fasting Challenge: How to receive manifestation of answers

How to Have Outrageous Financial Abundance In No Time:Biblical Principles For Immediate And Overwhelming Financial Success

5 Bible Promises, Prayers and Decrees That Will Give You The Best Year Ever: A book for Shaping Every Year Successfully plus devotional (Book Of Promises 1)

Influencing The Unseen Realm: How to Influence The Spirit Realm for Victory in The Physical Realm(Spiritual Success Books)

Prayer That Works: Taking Responsibility For Answered Prayer

Healing The Sick In Five Minutes:How Anyone Can Heal Any Sickness

The Financial Miracle Prayer

The Best Secret To Answered Prayer

The Believer's Authority(Authority Of The Believer,Power And Authority Of The Believer)

The Healing Miracle Prayer

I Shall Not Die: Secrets To Long Life And Overcoming The Fear of Death

Three Straightforward Steps To Outrageous Financial Abundance: Personal Finance (Finance Made Easy Book 1)

Prayers For Financial Miracles: And 3 Ways To Receive Answers Quickly

Book: 3 Point Blueprint For Building Strong Faith: Spiritual:Religious:Christian:Motivational

How To Stop Sinning Effortlessly

The Power Of Faith-Filled Words

All Sin Is Paid For: An Eye Opening Book

Be Happy Now:No More Depression

The Ultimate Christian: How To Win In Every Life Situation: A book full of Revelations

Books:How To Be Free From Sicknesses And Diseases(Divine Health): Divine Health Scriptures

Multiply Your Personal Income In Less Than 30 Days

Ultimate Method To Memorize The Bible Quickly: (How To Learn Scripture Memorization)

Overcoming Emotional Abuse

Passing Exams The Easy Way: 90% and above in exams (Learning Simplified)

Books:Goal Setting For Those In A Hurry To Achieve Fast

Do Something Lest You Do Nothing

Financial Freedom:My Personal Blue-Print Made Easy For Men And Women

Why Men Go To Hell

Budgeting Tools And How My Budget Makes Me More Money

How To Raise Capital In 72 Hours: Quickly and Effectively Raise Capital Easily in Unconventional Ways (Finance Made Easy)

How To Love Unconditionally

Financial Independence: The Simple Path I Used To Wealth

Finding Happiness: The Story Of John Miller: A Christian Fiction

Finance Made Easy (2 Book Series)

[Click here to see my author page](#)

Manufactured by Amazon.ca
Bolton, ON